MESSAGING WITH GOD

https://inflection-studios.com/shop/

ISBN 978-1-7335119-1-9

DEAR CHILD,

Of everything I created, YOU are my treasure. My heart beats for you and your heart beats for me. There is a reason you crave LOVE . You were never meant to be alone or separate from ME. Every day I want to reveal my love for you. All I need is an open and willing heart.

The life I have given you is an adventure with plenty of UPS and DOWNS. Remember that I AM always with you. There will never be a time where I AM not beside you. You are mine.

FRIENDS

I want to be your closest friend. Write down what is going on with you, and listen to what I have to say. I can't wait to hear from you!

I love you so much,

DATE: ____________________

What are you thinking about?

How does that make you feel?

How do you think I feel about it?

DATE: ______________________

What's going on?

Tell me more...

What do you hear me saying to you?

DATE: ____________________

Tell me about your day.

How do you feel?

Write down how I feel about you.

GOD

DATE: ____________________

What is something that bothers you?

What do you want to happen?

What do you think I want to happen?

DATE: ____________________

How are you feeling right now?

Why?

I care about your feelings. Listen to what I think about you...

Before you were born, I personally designed you while you were in your mother's tummy. I made you special and unique. You are the only one like you on the whole earth. I think you're awesome! You are my special creation!

BIBLE TREASURE HUNT:

Psalm 100:3; Psalm 119:13-16; Psalm 119:73

(Write the verses below.)

Blast
OFF WITH
THE Bible

WRITE OR DRAW YOURSELF THE WAY I SEE YOU: 

DATE: ______________________

What are you thinking about?

How does that make you feel?

How do you think I feel about it?

DATE: ____________________

What's going on?

Tell me more...

What do you hear me saying to you?

DATE: ______________________

Tell me about your day.

How do you feel?

Write down how I feel about you.

DATE: ____________________

What is something that bothers you?

What do you want to happen?

What do you think I want to happen?

DATE: ________________

How are you feeling right now?

Why?

I care about your feelings. Listen to what I think about you...

GOD

I am always watching over you, even though you don't see me. If you ever need my help, call me. I can help you with anything. Just whisper, "Jesus, help me," and I'll be right there!

BIBLE TREASURE HUNT:

Psalm 32:8; Proverbs 15:3; Psalm 91:15; Psalm 35:17

(Write the verses below.)

Blast
OFF WITH
THE Bible

WRITE DOWN SOME THINGS YOU WANT ME TO HELP YOU WITH:

1.

GOD

DATE: ____________________

What are you thinking about?

How does that make you feel?

How do you think I feel about it?

DATE: ______________________

What's going on?

Tell me more...

What do you hear me saying to you?

DATE: ______

Tell me about your day.

How do you feel?

Write down how I feel about you.

GOD

DATE: ____________________

What is something that bothers you?

What do you want to happen?

What do you think I want to happen?

DATE: ______

How are you feeling right now?

Why?

I care about your feelings. Listen to what I think about you...

GOD

Do you see the beautiful world I made for you to enjoy? Sunshine, cool clouds, stars, mountains, oceans, desert, flowers, snow, all kinds of animals. I created all of those things and more!

BIBLE TREASURE HUNT:

Psalm 24:1; Isaiah 45:12; Psalm 33:6; Genesis 1:1-28

(Write the verses below.)

Blast
OFF WITH
THE Bible

WRITE OR DRAW SOME OF YOUR FAVORITE THINGS I'VE CREATED THAT YOU ENJOY:

DATE: ____________________

What are you thinking about?

How does that make you feel?

How do you think I feel about it?

DATE: ____________________

What's going on?

Tell me more...

What do you hear me saying to you?

DATE: ______________________

Tell me about your day.

How do you feel?

Write down how I feel about you.

GOD

DATE: ____________________

What is something that bothers you?

What do you want to happen?

What do you think I want to happen?

GOD

DATE: ____________________

How are you feeling right now?

Why?

I care about your feelings. Listen to what I think about you...

People are my #1 favorite creation. I want to have people as my closest friends. It makes me sad that many people reject me and do sinful things that separate us. But my son, Jesus, came to earth to bring us together. He died to take the punishment for all of your sins. If you ask Jesus to forgive you of all you've done wrong, I will forgive you too. Then we can be close friends--forever.

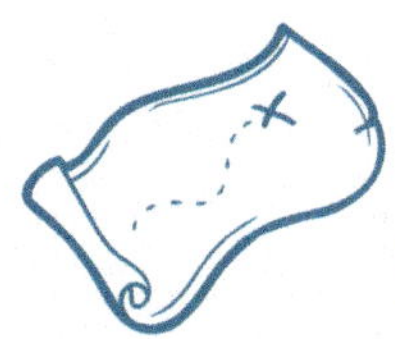

BIBLE TREASURE HUNT:

Ecclesiastes 7:20; Romans 5:8; Romans 3:23-24; John 3:16; 1 John 1:9; 1 John 4:9

(Write the verses below.)

Blast
OFF WITH
THE Bible

WHAT IS YOUR RELATIONSHIP WITH JESUS LIKE?

DATE: ______________________

What are you thinking about?

How does that make you feel?

How do you think I feel about it?

DATE: ____________________

What's going on?

Tell me more...

What do you hear me saying to you?

DATE: ______________________

Tell me about your day.

How do you feel?

Write down how I feel about you.

GOD

DATE: ____________________

What is something that bothers you?

What do you want to happen?

What do you think I want to happen?

DATE: ____________________

How are you feeling right now?

Why?

I care about your feelings. Listen to what I think about you...

Be careful about what you watch and listen to. Everything you put inside your mind will become part of you. You only want GOOD things in you. It doesn't matter what anyone else is doing. I want you to be filled with goodness and peace. Ask me if something is GOOD to watch or listen to.

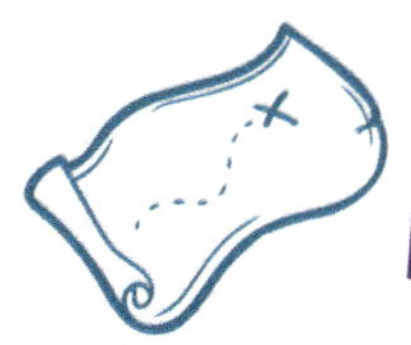

BIBLE TREASURE HUNT:

1 Corinthians 6:19; Psalm 34:14; Philippians 4:8; Colossians 3:17

(Write the verses below.)

Blast
OFF WITH
THE Bible

WRITE DOWN SOME THINGS THAT WILL FILL YOU WITH GOOD INSIDE: 

1.

GOD

DATE:

What are you thinking about?

How does that make you feel?

How do you think I feel about it?

DATE: ______________________

What's going on?

Tell me more...

What do you hear me saying to you?

DATE: ____________________

Tell me about your day.

How do you feel?

Write down how I feel about you.

GOD

DATE:

What is something that bothers you?

What do you want to happen?

What do you think I want to happen?

DATE: ______________________

How are you feeling right now?

Why?

I care about your feelings. Listen to what I think about you...

Life can be stressful, frustrating, or upsetting. But I want my children to be happy! Whenever you feel stressed or upset inside, tell me about it. You can whisper to me or write to me. Then close your eyes and listen... I will tell you what to do. I will give you my peace and happiness. I really want you to be happy. Let me help you!

BIBLE TREASURE HUNT:

Philippians 4;6-7; 1 Peter 5:7; Isaiah 41:13

(Write the verses below.)

Blast
OFF WITH
THE Bible

WHAT MAKES YOU FEEL STRESSED?

DATE: ____________________

What are you thinking about?

How does that make you feel?

How do you think I feel about it?

DATE: ____________________

What's going on?

Tell me more...

What do you hear me saying to you?

GOD

DATE: ____________________

Tell me about your day.

How do you feel?

Write down how I feel about you.

DATE: ______________________

What is something that bothers you?

What do you want to happen?

What do you think I want to happen?

GOD

DATE: ______

How are you feeling right now?

Why?

I care about your feelings. Listen to what I think about you...

There are a lot of scary things in the world. But I'm WAY stronger than anything or anyone, and I'm on your side. If you have nightmares or get scared any time, call for me. Say, "Jesus, save me" and I will! Everyone who calls on my name will be saved. Remember my name, JESUS, is stronger than all evil.

Psalm 34:17; Psalm 121:7-8; 2 Thessalonians 3:3; Romans 10:13; Philippians 2:9-11

(Write the verses below.)

Blast
OFF WITH
THE
Bible

WHAT SCARES YOU?

DATE: ____________________

What are you thinking about?

How does that make you feel?

How do you think I feel about it?

GOD

DATE: ______________________

What's going on?

Tell me more...

What do you hear me saying to you?

DATE: ____________________

Tell me about your day.

How do you feel?

Write down how I feel about you.

GOD

DATE: ____________________

What is something that bothers you?

What do you want to happen?

What do you think I want to happen?

GOD

DATE: ________________

How are you feeling right now?

Why?

I care about your feelings. Listen to what I think about you...

Do you know what makes me happy? When you sing to me. When you talk with me. When you treat other people with kindness. When you say good things. I love when you behave like this!

Do you know what hurts my heart? When you ignore me. When you are mean to others. When you have a bad attitude. When you curse or lie or complain. I don't want you to behave like this at all.

BIBLE TREASURE HUNT:

Psalm 96:1-2; 1 John 4:7; Ephesians 5:1-4

(Write the verses below.)

Blast
OFF WITH
THE Bible

WHAT BEHAVIORS CAN YOU CHANGE TO MAKE ME HAPPY? (YOU WILL BE HAPPY TOO!)

1.

The next few pages are for you to draw, write, color, and be creative. I enjoy watching you and listening to you. I really, really love you!

WRITE DOWN SOME OF YOUR FAVORITE VERSES:

1.

BIG IDEAS

Made in the USA
Las Vegas, NV
22 November 2024